# CITY FUN

Modern Curriculum Press
**BEGINNING TO READ** Series

# CITY FUN

**Margaret Hillert**

Illustrated by Barbara Corey

**MODERN CURRICULUM PRESS**
Cleveland • Toronto

**Library of Congress Cataloging in Publication Data**

Hillert, Margaret.
  City fun.

  SUMMARY: As two girls explore the city, they watch buildings being torn down and built, ride the subway, visit the park, watch a parade, play games, and visit the library.
  [1. City and town life—Fiction]    I. Corey, Barbara.    II. Title
PZ7.H558Ci    [E]    80-14564

ISBN 0-8136-5571-4 Paperback
ISBN 0-8136-5071-2 Hardbound

Library of Congress Catalog Card Number: 80-14564

15  16  17  18  19  20     99  98  97

I like it here.
I like what I see.
I like what I do.
I have fun.

See what we can play.
We have to jump.
Jump, jump, jump.

And we can do this.
Look at us go.
We have to work at this.

Here is something
to look at.
See it go up.
Up, up, up.

And look at this.
It will come down.
Down, down, down.

Away, away, away.
We will ride away.
What a good ride.

I see something.
Red ones, yellow ones, blue ones.
I will get one.
Here is one for me.

I want this, too.
I like this.
It is good.

Now see what we can do.
It is fun to do this.
Look out. Look out.

Oh, look at that.
Here it comes.
What fun. What fun.

Look at this.
See what I can do.
I like it.
I like it.

It is fun up here.
Way, way up here.
And I like to look down.

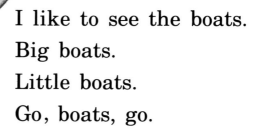

I like to see the boats.
Big boats.
Little boats.
Go, boats, go.

Oh, what fun!
Up and down.
Up and down.

We can go up and down, too.
We can jump, jump, jump.
1 and 2 and 3 and 4 . . .

Here is a man.
What will he do?
What can he do for us?

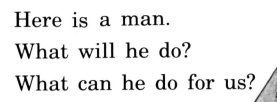

Oh, oh, oh.
Look at this.
Come in. Come in.
It is good in here.

And here comes something.
We like this.
We will get something
good to eat.

Come here. Come here.
Guess what we can do in here.
Guess. Guess.

We can get something.
You will like it.
You can take it with you.

I like it out here.
It is fun to sit here.
It is fun to do
what we do.

**Margaret Hillert,** author and poet, has written many books for young readers. She is a former first-grade teacher and lives in Birmingham, Michigan.

*City Fun* uses the 58 words listed below.

| | | | |
|---|---|---|---|
| a | get | man | take |
| and | go | me | that |
| at | good | | the |
| away | guess | now | this |
| | | | to |
| big | have | oh | too |
| blue | he | one(s) | |
| boats | here | out | up |
| | | | us |
| can | I | play | |
| come(s) | in | | want |
| | is | red | way |
| do | it | ride | we |
| down | | | what |
| | jump | see | will |
| eat | | sit | with |
| | like | something | work |
| for | little | | |
| fun | look | | yellow |
| | | | you |